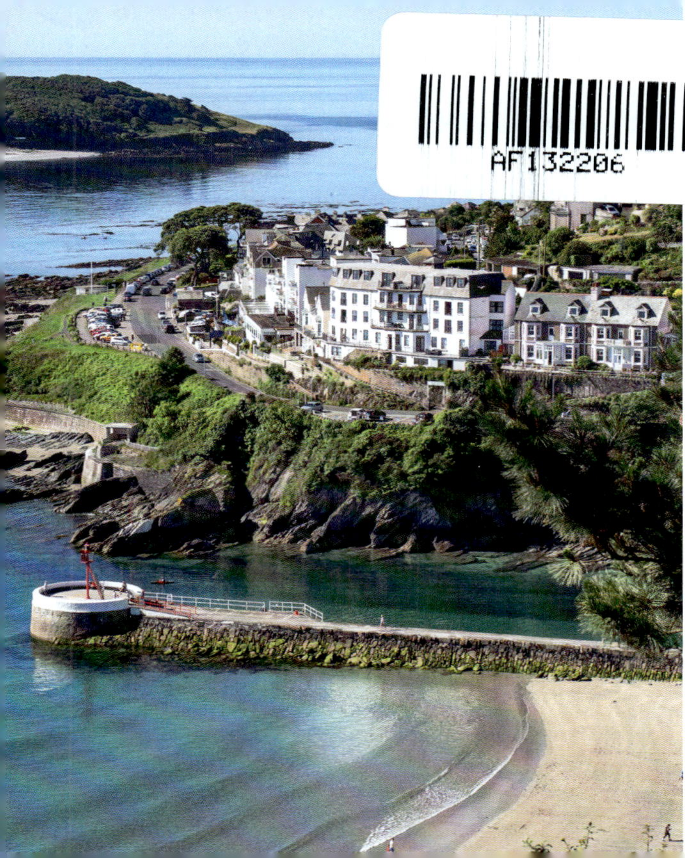

FAVOURITE CORNISH RECIPES

compiled by
June Kittow

I love thee, Cornwall, and will ever,
And hope to see thee once again,
For why? - thine equal knew I never,
For honest minds and active men.
⠀⠀⠀⠀⠀⠀⠀⠀⠀⠀⠀⠀⠀⠀⠀⠀⠀⠀⠀Thomas Freeman

Index

- Apple Cake 27
- Apple Meringue 46
- Bacon and Egg Pie 43
- Baked Herrings 45
- Buttered Crab 8
- Chocolate Tarts 38
- Cornish Chicken Pie 40
- Cornish Clotted Cream 21
- Cornish Heavy Cake 47
- Cornish Junket 30
- Cornish Pasty 3
- Cornish Potato Cake 10
- Cornish Saffron Cake 37
- Cornish Splits 5
- Cornish Under Roast 18
- Crab with Devil Sauce 35
- Easter Cakes 31
- Figgie Hobbin 31
- Ginger Fairings 29
- Individual Mutton Pies 26
- Ley Mill Lemon Pudding 39
- Luncheon Cake 23
- Marinated Pilchards 16
- Masked Eggs with Asparagus 15
- Mutton and Turnip Pie 6
- Pea Soup 22
- Penzance Cake 13
- Potato Omelette 30
- Railway Pudding 14
- Rich Plum Cake 34
- Roast Sea Bass 32
- Sausage Roly-Poly 11
- Special Christmas Pudding 42
- Star Gazey Pie 24
- Store Cake 7
- Yeast Cake 19

Front Cover: Mousehole Harbour, Back Cover: Cornish Tin Mine, Title Page: Looe, Cornwall

Printed & published by Dorrigo, Manchester, England © Copyright

All rights reserved. No part of this publication may be reproduced, stored in a retrieval system or transmitted, in any form or by means, electronic, mechanical, photocopying or otherwise. Images: Adobe Stock, Recipes: J Salmon Ltd

Cornish Pasty

The better quality the beef and the more finely cut the vegetables, the tastier the pasty.

PASTRY
1 lb. plain flour   Good pinch of salt   5 oz. lard   Water to mix
FILLING
1 lb. best quality lean beef   ½ lb. peeled potatoes   ½ lb. peeled swede
1 small onion, peeled   Salt and pepper   Butter   Beaten egg to glaze

Set oven to 400°F or Mark 6. Grease and flour a baking sheet. To make the pastry, sift the flour and salt into a bowl and rub in the lard until the mixture resembles breadcrumbs. Then mix in just sufficient water until the pastry leaves the side of the bowl cleanly. Divide the pastry into 4 equal pieces and roll each piece into a round about 7 to 8 inches diameter on a lightly floured surface. For the filling, cut the beef into small cubes, about ¼ inch, removing all fat. Cut up the potatoes into small irregular pieces and similarly the swede and onion. On each round of pastry put a share of the vegetables and season well with salt and pepper. Then add a share of the meat with a good knob of butter and another sprinkle of pepper. Dampen the edge of the pastry and bring up from both sides with floured hands to envelop the filling. Pinch the edges together and crimp firmly to seal. Brush with beaten egg and cook on the baking sheet for about ¾ hour until golden brown. Makes 4 pasties.

Cornish Splits

These little yeast cakes are delicious served split and buttered and spread with homemade jam and Cornish cream. If served with black treacle and cream they are called "Thunder and Lightning".

1 lb. plain flour	1 teaspoon salt
1 oz. fresh yeast	2 oz. lard or margarine
1 teaspoon sugar	½ pint warm milk

Set oven to 400°F or Mark 6. Mix the yeast and sugar to a liquid, add some warm milk and set aside to sponge. Meantime, sieve the flour and salt into a bowl and rub in the fat. Add the yeast mixture and the rest of the milk and mix together to a soft dough. Turn out on to a lightly floured surface and knead well. Replace in the bowl, cover, put in a warm place and leave to rise until doubled in size. Knead again and shape the dough into small round cakes, or buns. Put on to a floured baking sheet, leave to prove again, then bake for about 15 to 20 minutes until browned on top.

Bude, Cornwall

Mutton and Turnip Pie

This pie from St. Germans on the Lynher River traditionally made a good and satisfying meal after a day's hunting.

**2 lb. lean mutton (or lamb)   2 onions, peeled
1 lb. turnips, peeled   Salt and pepper
1 oz butter   1 oz. flour
1 dessertspoon chopped fresh parsley
¾ lb. puff pastry**

Set oven to 400°F or Mark 6. Cut the mutton or lamb into 1 inch cubes, discarding all fat and gristle. Cut the onions into quarters and slice the turnips. Put the meat and vegetables into a saucepan, season well and cover with cold water. Bring to the boil, cover the pan and simmer for 2 hours. Remove from the heat, pour off the liquid, retain and set aside. Allow the meat mixture to cool. Make a roux with the butter and flour and gradually add the retained liquid over a gentle heat to thicken and make a rich gravy. Put the meat and vegetables into a pie dish, sprinkle with the chopped parsley and three-quarter fill the dish with gravy. Save the rest of the gravy to re-heat and serve separately. Cover with a pastry lid, decorate with leaves and a rose, make a steam hole and bake for about 25 minutes. Serves 4 to 5.

Store Cake

A fruit cake which is useful to have as a stand-by in the cupboard to use as required.

8 oz. margarine	6 oz. sultanas
8 oz. caster sugar	3 oz. glacé cherries, quartered
4 eggs, beaten	3 oz. chopped mixed peel
12 oz. plain flour	2 oz. blanched almonds, chopped
6 oz. currants	Grated rind of 1 lemon

Set oven to 350°F or Mark 4. Grease and line an 8-inch cake tin. In a bowl, cream together the margarine and sugar until light and fluffy. Beat in the eggs gradually, fold in the flour and add the dried fruit, glacé cherries, peel, almonds and lemon rind. Put into the tin and bake for 2½ hours or until a skewer inserted comes out clean. Leave to cool in the tin and turn out on to a wire rack.

Buttered Crab

This makes a nice starter; a change from paté.

2 large boiled crabs	½ pint white wine
2 anchovy fillets	Salt and white pepper
1 cup white breadcrumbs	3 tablespoons melted butter
Pinch of nutmeg	Slices of buttered toast

Mash the anchovy fillets and work in with the breadcrumbs and nutmeg. Add the wine and season to taste. Put the mixture into a pan, bring gently to the boil and simmer for 5 minutes. Flake the meat from the crabs, mix with the melted butter and add to the hot wine mixture. Cook gently for 4 minutes then arrange on a hot serving dish surrounded by strips of buttered toast. Serve with a side salad. Serves 6.

Polperro, Cornwall

Cornish Potato Cake

*Numerous regional variations from all over the British Isles
have evolved for these tasty and filling 'scones'.*

**1½ - 2 lb. potatoes, peeled   1 teaspoon salt
6 oz. shredded suet   Flour to bind into a stiff paste**

Set oven to 350°F or Mark 4. Grease a baking tin. Boil and mash the potatoes and, whilst hot, add the suet and salt and mix in enough flour to make a dough of a firm consistency. Press out with the hands on a lightly floured surface to a rectangle about 1-inch thickness. Put in the greased tin, mark deeply into squares and bake for about 1 hour until golden brown. Allow to cool, divide into cakes and eat either plain or buttered or served hot with gravy.

Sausage Roly-Poly

An easy-to-make steamed suet roll and a satisfying meal.

1 lb. self-raising flour
4 oz. shredded suet
Cold water to mix
1 lb. sausage meat
1 onion, finely sliced
1 potato, very thinly sliced
Salt and pepper

In a bowl, mix the flour and suet with just sufficient water to produce a stiff dough. Roll out the dough on a lightly floured surface to about ½-inch thickness. Spread the sausage meat liberally over the dough, add a layer of finely sliced onion and then a layer of very thinly sliced potato. Season with salt and pepper. Roll up tightly and tie in a well-floured pudding cloth, leaving plenty of room for the pudding to swell. Boil for 2½ hours. Serve with a green vegetable. Serves 4 to 6.

Penzance Cake

A very fruity cake made with a plain mixture.

- 1 lb. plain flour
- ½ teaspoon bicarbonate of soda
- 4 oz. butter, softened
- 2 teaspoons ground cinnamon
- 1 lb. currants
- 8 oz. chopped crystallised ginger
- 4 oz. chopped mixed peel
- 2 eggs, beaten
- 5 fl.oz. tepid milk

Set oven to 350° F or Mark 4. Grease and line a 9 to 10-inch cake tin. Sift the flour and bicarbonate of soda into a bowl and rub in the butter until the mixture resembles breadcrumbs. Add the cinnamon, currants, ginger and mixed peel and mix to a soft consistency with the beaten eggs and milk. Put into the tin and bake for about 2 hours or until a skewer inserted comes out clean. Leave to cool in the tin and turn out on to a wire rack.

Saint Michael's Mount, Marazion, Cornwall

Railway Pudding

A baked pudding of lightly stewed apples sandwiched between layers of cake mixture.

1 lb. cooking apples   1 egg, beaten   2 oz. soft margarine
4 oz. self-raising flour   2 oz. caster sugar   ½ teacup milk

Set oven to 350°F or Mark 4. Grease a pie dish. Stew the apples for a short time only in very little water. In a bowl, cream together the margarine and sugar, beat in the egg, stir in the flour and mix to a batter with the milk. Pour a layer of batter into the pie dish, cover with the semi-stewed apples and pour over the rest of the batter. Bake for about 30 minutes until golden brown. Serves 4.

Masked Eggs with Asparagus

A very good hors-d'œuvre dish. An advantage is that everything can be prepared in advance and easily assembled about half an hour before the meal.

6 eggs
6 rounds of fried bread
2 tablespoons clotted cream
1 lb. asparagus
¼ pint mayonnaise

Poach the eggs softly and leave to drain. Fry the slices of bread and cut each to a round to fit an egg. Boil the asparagus for 3 or 4 minutes. Drain, then cut off the tips about 2-inches long and chop up the remainder of the edible parts. Mix the mayonnaise and cream together thoroughly. Place the rounds of bread on a flat serving dish or on individual hors-d'œuvre dishes. Lay an egg on each round of bread with 3 or 4 asparagus tips alongside each one and sprinkle around the chopped asparagus. Then pour the mayonnaise over each egg so it is covered and 'masked' and only the asparagus tips are showing.

Marinated Pilchards

*An ideal summer lunch or supper dish, served with crusty bread
or with a green or potato salad.*

6 pilchards (or mackerel)   **1 teaspoon brown sugar**
3 bay leaves   **¼ pint cold tea (no milk)**
10 peppercorns   **¼ pint vinegar**
4 cloves   **Pinch of salt**

Clean and fillet the fish. Cut up the flesh about 2 inches square and pack into a deep pudding basin. Put all the other ingredients into a saucepan and bring to the boil. Simmer for 2 or 3 minutes for the flavours to infuse. When ready, strain the liquid over the fish, cover with a saucer and leave in the refrigerator for 3 or 4 days. Serves 3 to 4.

St Ives, Cornwall

Cornish Under Roast

Steak, laid on a bed of vegetables in a roasting tin and cooked in the oven.
This recipe has the advantage of not requiring any cooking fat or oil.

1½ lb. steak (rump or as preferred) in one piece
Seasoned flour   ¼ swede (½ lb.), peeled
1 large carrot   1 large onion   Salt and pepper
2 lb. potatoes, peeled   ½ pint water or vegetable stock

Set oven to 375°F or Mark 5. Cut up the swede, carrot and onion into fairly small pieces and put into a roasting tin. Season lightly. Dust the steak, in one piece, with seasoned flour and lay on the vegetables. Cut the potatoes into halves and pack around the meat. Add ½-pint water and cook for ½ hour. Adjust the seasoning, reduce oven to 350°F or Mark 4 and continue to cook for another hour. Serve with a green vegetable. Serves 4 to 6.

Yeast Cake

This mixture can be used either to make a currant dough cake or individual currant buns.

1 oz. fresh yeast
2 oz. sugar
½ pint tepid milk
1 lb. plain flour
Pinch of salt
2 oz. butter, softened
2 oz. lard
4 oz. currants and/or sultanas
2 oz. chopped mixed peel

Set oven to 400°F or Mark 6. Grease a 7-inch cake tin or a baking sheet if making buns. Mix together the yeast and a teaspoon of the sugar, add the milk and set aside in a warm place to sponge. Sift the flour and salt into a bowl and rub in the fats until the mixture resembles breadcrumbs. Stir in the remaining sugar, the dried fruit and peel, then work in the yeast mixture and knead well. Return to the lightly greased or floured bowl and leave to rise in a warm place until doubled in size. Knock back, knead again and put into the tin or make into buns. Allow to prove in the warm for about 20 minutes. When risen, bake the cake for about 30 minutes or until a skewer inserted comes out clean; or bake the buns for about 15 to 20 minutes. Leave to cool and turn out on to a wire rack.

Cornish Clotted Cream

The richest cream of all, Cornish clotted cream is the main constituent of a 'cream tea' served with scones and home-made jam. It is wonderful served with all desserts.

2 pints very fresh full cream milk, preferably Jersey

Pour the milk into a wide-topped basin and leave to stand for a while, preferably up to 8 hours in the refrigerator, to allow the cream to rise to the top. Then stand the basin in a shallow pan of water and bring slowly to the boil. Continue simmering, as slowly as possible, for 2 or 3 hours until the cream has formed a rich, bubbly crust. Allow to cool for several hours, preferably in the refrigerator. Finally, skim off the clotted cream into a dish. This quantity of milk makes about 4 oz. of cream. Use up the remaining milk in the ordinary way; drink it by the glass when freshly skimmed or in tea or coffee or to make puddings, for example bread and butter pudding.

Fowey, Cornwall

Pea Soup

This recipe from North Cornwall is made with dried peas and mixed vegetables and is served with clotted cream.

1 lb. dried peas	1 leek, chopped
2 pints water	1 rasher of bacon, finely chopped
1 bay leaf	1 pint milk
1 sprig thyme	Salt and pepper
1 sprig mint	Chopped fresh mint
1 carrot, sliced	2 oz. clotted cream
1 onion, chopped	Croûtons

Soak the dried peas overnight in cold water. Next day, put the soaked peas into a large saucepan and add 2 pints of water. Add all the other ingredients except the milk and seasoning. Bring to the boil and simmer for 2 hours. Liquidize and return to the saucepan. Heat the milk nearly to boiling point, add to the purée and season to taste. Re-heat and sprinkle in a little chopped mint. Add a dessertspoon of clotted cream to each serving and garnish with croûtons. Serves 6.

Luncheon Cake

A light sherry-flavoured fruit cake which is nice eaten on its own or with a glass of fortified wine; a recipe from Mrs. Griffiths of Truro.

6 oz. butter, softened
6 oz. caster sugar
3 eggs
1 lb. plain flour
1 dessertspoon baking powder
2 teaspoons salt
1 teacup warm milk and water mixed
8 oz. sultanas
2 oz. chopped mixed peel
½ wine glass sweet sherry

Set oven to 375° F or Mark 5. Grease an 8-inch round cake tin. In a bowl, cream together the butter and sugar until light and fluffy. Add the eggs one at a time, beating to a creamy mixture. Sieve together the flour, baking powder and salt and gradually stir into the butter mixture alternately with the milk/water, a little at a time. Just before all the flour is used up, add the sultanas and peel, then the last of the flour and the sherry and mix well. Put into the tin and bake for 1 hour, then reduce oven to 350°F or Mark 4 and continue for about another hour or until a skewer inserted comes out clean. Leave to cool in the tin then turn out on to a wire rack.

Star Gazey Pie

This renowned Cornish pie is particularly linked with Mousehole. The name derives from the way the fish heads overlap the sides of dish and point heavenwards.

**6 pilchards (or 8 large sardines)   1 small onion, finely chopped
8 oz. shortcrust pastry   1 egg, beaten   6 oz. brown breadcrumbs
3 hardboiled eggs, chopped   1 teaspoon ground cloves   4 teaspoons single cream
1 teaspoon allspice   4 tablespoons chopped parsley
Freshly ground black pepper   Beaten egg for glazing**

Set oven to 425° F or Mark 7. Gut, clean and bone the fish, cut off the tail fins but leave on the heads. Wash the fish, pat dry, then open out. Make the stuffing with breadcrumbs, cloves, spice and pepper, mixed with the chopped onions and bound together with beaten egg. Fill the opened fish with stuffing, close up, reshape and leave in a cool place. Grease a 9 to 10-inch flat pie-dish or pie-plate. Spread any remaining stuffing over the dish and arrange the stuffed fish like the spokes of a wheel with heads on the rim and tails in the centre. Cover with chopped hard-boiled egg, cream, parsley and pepper; finish covering with the rest of the pastry and pinch the two layers firmly together between the heads but roll back the pastry round the heads to reveal their eyes gazing starwards. Brush with beaten egg. Bake for 15 minutes, reduce oven to 350°F or Mark 4 and continue for a further 20 minutes until the pie is golden brown. Serves 6.

Mousehole Harbour, Cornwall

Individual Mutton Pies

These straightforward meat pies, made nowadays more usually from lamb, are simple to make and provide a good meal.

2 lb. shortcrust pastry	2 tablespoons chopped fresh parsley
1½ lb. lean mutton or lamb	1½ pints well-seasoned gravy
2 onions, finely chopped	2 egg yolks for glazing

Set oven to 325°F or Mark 3. Grease 8 to 10 deep patty tins. Roll out the pastry on a lightly floured surface and use to line the tins. A good way to do this is to cut rough circles of pastry and mould them over the base of a tumbler the size of the tin. Slip off the pastry and fit into the tin, then trim the top edge. Remove all fat from the meat and cut into about ¼-inch cubes. Mix the meat and onions together and fill each of the pies. Add a little chopped parsley and ¾-fill with gravy. Cover with pastry lids, make a steam hole and brush liberally with egg yolk. Cook for about 1 hour until well browned. Serve hot with a garnish of parsley. Makes 8 to 10 pies.

Apple Cake

*A dessert cake covered with sliced apple, baked and served with clotted cream;
a recipe from Mrs. Bray of Wadebridge.*

6 oz. self-raising flour
Pinch of salt
3 oz. butter, softened
3 oz. sultanas
3 oz. caster sugar
2 eggs, beaten
1 cooking apple
½ teaspoon ground cinnamon
1 teaspoon granulated sugar

Set oven to 400°F or Mark 6. Grease an 8-inch square shallow baking tin. Put the flour and salt into a mixing bowl and rub in the butter until the mixture resembles breadcrumbs. Add the sultanas and caster sugar and mix together with the beaten eggs. Put the mixture into the tin. Core and peel the apple, cut into slices and arrange over the cake mixture. Sprinkle the cinnamon and granulated sugar over the top and bake for 30 minutes. Serve hot or cold with clotted cream.

Ginger Fairings

These spicy ginger biscuits were traditionally sold at Cornish country fairs and today are popular with visitors to the county.

- 4 oz. plain flour
- 1 teaspoon baking powder
- 1 teaspoon bicarbonate of soda
- 1 teaspoon ground cinnamon
- 1 teaspoon ground ginger
- 1 teaspoon mixed spice
- 1 oz. grated lemon peel
- 2 oz. brown sugar
- 2 oz. butter or margarine
- 2 tablespoons golden syrup, warmed

Set oven to 350°F or Mark 4. Grease a baking sheet. Mix the baking powder, bicarbonate of soda, the spices and lemon peel together in a bowl, sieve in the flour and add the sugar. Mix thoroughly. Rub in the butter or margarine until the mixture resembles breadcrumbs. Add the warmed syrup, using the fingers to combine to a smooth paste, then roll the final mix, with floured hands, into small balls, each about the size of a walnut. Place the balls on the baking sheet, leaving plenty of room between each one. Cook for about 15 minutes then reduce temperature to 325°F or Mark 3 and finish cooking for 5 to 10 minutes so that the biscuits sink and crack into their familiar form. Transfer to a wire rack to cool.

Kynance Cove, The Lizard, Cornwall

Cornish Junket

Junkets are popular in Cornwall, particularly when made with brandy and clotted cream!

**1 pint milk, preferably full-cream   1 dessertspoon sugar
2 sugar lumps rubbed on a lemon
2½ fl.oz. brandy   1 tablespoon rennet   Clotted cream**

Warm the milk to blood heat, add the sugar and stir in the sugar lumps. Pour the brandy into a serving dish, add the milk junket and stir in the rennet. Put into the refrigerator to set and, when set, cover with clotted cream. Serves 3 to 4.

Potato Omelette

A quick and substantial supper dish. A good way to use up left-over boiled potatoes.

**8 oz. boiled potatoes (left-over or newly prepared)   3 eggs, beaten
A little chopped fresh parsley   Salt and pepper   1 oz. butter**

If necessary, first boil 8 oz. of peeled potatoes and leave to cool. When ready, beat the eggs thoroughly, season and mix in the parsley. Cut the potatoes into small pieces and add to the eggs. Melt the butter in a frying pan and when just beginning to smoke faintly, pour in the egg mixture. Cook over a moderate heat until golden brown on the underside. Fold over and serve on a hot plate.

Easter Cakes

Soft, fruit-filled biscuits, flavoured with cinnamon and with a sugary topping.

**3 oz. butter, softened   3 oz. caster sugar   Pinch of ground cinnamon
6 oz. plain flour   2 oz. currants   1 egg, beaten**

Set oven to 375°F or Mark 5. Grease a baking sheet. In a bowl, beat the butter to a cream, mix in the sugar, cinnamon and flour and then the currants. Mix to a stiff paste with sufficient of the beaten egg. Roll out thinly on a lightly floured surface and cut into rounds with a tumbler or cutter. Sprinkle with sugar and place on the baking sheet. Bake for about 10 minutes until golden.

Figgie Hobbin

A dried fig slice made with suet and lard.

**8 oz. plain flour   ¾ teaspoon baking powder   2 oz. chopped suet
2 oz. lard   8 oz. dried figs, chopped   2-3 fl.oz. milk**

Set oven to 400° F or Mark 6. Grease a baking sheet. Sift the flour and baking powder into a bowl, rub in the suet and lard and mix in the chopped figs. Blend in sufficient milk to produce a stiff dough. Roll out on a floured surface to ½-inch thickness and cut into 4 inch squares. Put on the baking sheet, score the surfaces lightly with a knife and bake for about 30 minutes until golden.

Roast Sea Bass

This round, somewhat salmon-like fish is caught off the coast of Cornwall.
Large bass, about 3 to 3½ lbs. if available, have the best flavour.
This recipe is equally suitable for sea bream.

1 large sea bass or 3 fish approx 1-1¼ lb. each
3 oz. suet   1 tablespoon chopped fresh parsley
4 oz. fresh white breadcrumbs   Sea salt
Milk to mix

PARSLEY BUTTER
2 oz. butter   1 tablespoon finely chopped fresh parsley

Set oven to 400°F or Mark 6. Clean and de-scale the fish (by the fishmonger if preferred). Keep back 1 oz. suet (for basting) and thoroughly mix the rest with the chopped parsley and breadcrumbs and with a pinch of salt. Moisten with a little milk. Stuff the fish with this mixture and put into a greased baking dish. Sprinkle with the remaining suet and season generously with salt. Bake for about 20 to 25 minutes until golden brown, basting frequently and adding more suet if it seems at all dry. Serve with parsley butter made of 2 oz. butter and 1 tablespoon finely chopped parsley, well blended together. Serves 3 to 4.

Mevagissey Harbour, Cornwall

Rich Plum Cake

An extremely fruity cake which is suitable for a special occasion.

- 8 oz. butter
- 8 oz. caster sugar
- 6 medium eggs, lightly beaten
- 8 oz. currants
- 8 oz. raisins
- 8 oz. sultanas
- 4 oz. glacé cherries, halved
- 8 oz. plain flour
- 8 oz. chopped mixed peel
- 8 oz. almonds, blanched and chopped
- 2 tablespoons rum or brandy
- 1 tablespoon black coffee

Set oven to 325°F or Mark 3. Grease a 9-inch round cake tin. In a bowl, cream together the butter and sugar until light and fluffy. Stir in the lightly beaten eggs one at a time with a teaspoon of flour after the third egg. Beat thoroughly. Mix all the dried fruit together with half the flour. Stir the rest of the flour, together with the peel and almonds, into the egg and butter mixture. Then add the floured fruit, the rum or brandy and the coffee. Put in the tin and bake for 2½ hours or longer, until a skewer inserted comes out clean. To prevent the sides from burning, tie a band of brown paper round the outside of the tin before baking. Leave to cool in the tin and turn out on to a wire rack.

Crab with Devil Sauce

Grilled crab meat with a hot, spicy cream sauce. A lovely summer supper dish, especially when eaten looking out to sea!

- **2 medium size crabs**
- **¼ pint double cream**
- **1 teaspoon anchovy paste**
- **¼ teaspoon English mustard powder**
- **1 tablespoon Worcestershire sauce**
- **1 tablespoon mushroom ketchup**
- **Dash of cayenne pepper**
- **Salt and pepper**

Whip the cream and mix in all the ingredients except the crab meat, until all is thick and creamy. Put the meat from the 2 crabs into an ovenproof dish and cover with the sauce. Grill under a medium grill or bake in a hot oven (450°F or Mark 8) for 5 to 10 minutes. Serve with wedges of lemon and a side salad and freshly baked Cornish Splits.

Cornish Saffron Cake

This old English cake or sweetbread which originated in Cornwall, is made from saffron-flavoured yeast dough with currants and candied peel.

1 teaspoon saffron strands	6 oz. butter, softened
1-2 tablespoons boiling water	2 sachets 'easy-blend' yeast
1 lb. strong flour	3 oz. sugar
½ teaspoon salt	6 oz. currants
½ teaspoon ground nutmeg	2 oz. chopped candied peel
6 fl.oz. lukewarm milk	

Steep the saffron in the boiled water. Grease a 2 lb. loaf tin. Sift the flour, salt and nutmeg into a bowl and rub in the butter until the mixture resembles breadcrumbs. Then add the yeast, sugar, currants and peel and mix well. Make a well in the mixture, add the saffron water and sufficient of the warm milk to produce a soft dough. Turn out on a floured surface and knead well for about 10 minutes. Put in a clean bowl, cover and leave in a warm place to rise; the heavy dough is somewhat slow to rise. When risen, knead again and put into the tin. Leave in the warm to prove. Set oven to 375°F or Mark 5. Bake for about 40 minutes then reduce oven to 350°F or Mark 4 and bake for about a further 50 minutes until a skewer inserted comes out clean. Leave to cool in the tin for 15 minutes then turn out on to a wire rack. Serve sliced and buttered.

Truro Cathedral

Chocolate Tarts

The chocolate and almond filling makes these little tarts into a delicious tea-time treat.

8 oz. shortcrust pastry   4 oz. caster sugar
3 oz. ground almonds   2 oz. plain chocolate
1 egg, beaten

Set oven to 400°F or Mark 6. Grease 12 patty tins. Roll out the pastry thinly on a lightly floured surface and cut out to line the patty tins. Mix the ground almonds and sugar together in a bowl. Melt the chocolate in a bowl over a pan of boiling water. Gradually stir the beaten egg and the melted chocolate, alternately, into the almond/sugar mixture. Fill the pastry cases with the mixture and bake for about 15 minutes until the pastry is golden.

Ley Mill Lemon Pudding

A very light, lemon-flavoured dessert made with breadcrumbs and milk.

2 oz. fresh white breadcrumbs **Grated rind and juice of ½ lemon**
½ pint fresh milk **Sugar to taste**
1 large egg, separated

Set oven to 350°F or Mark 4. Grease a pie dish. Put the breadcrumbs and milk into a bowl and leave to soak for at least one hour before cooking. When fully soaked, mix in the lemon rind and juice, add sufficient sugar to taste and mix in the egg yolk. Beat the egg white stiffly and then fold in to the mixture very carefully so it does not curdle. Put into the pie dish and bake for about ½ hour until golden brown on top. Serves 2 to 3.

Cornish Chicken Pie

The caudle or cream-and-egg mixture is poured in at the end of the cooking.

3-4 chicken breasts, skinned   1-2 oz. butter   2 onions, chopped
½ oz. chopped fresh parsley   Pinch of ground mace   Pinch of ground nutmeg
¼ pint full cream milk   Salt and pepper
¾ lb puff pastry   1 egg, beaten   ¼ pint Cornish or double cream

Set oven to 425°F or Mark 7. Grease a 1½ pint pie dish. Cut the chicken breasts into 1 inch pieces and lightly fry in butter until just coloured. Spread the pieces over the base of the pie dish. Lightly fry the onions in the remaining butter to soften, add the parsley, mace and nutmeg and the milk and bring slowly to the boil. Reduce the heat and simmer for 2 to 3 minutes, stirring to deglaze the pan. Pour the milk/onion mixture over the chicken pieces and season well. Roll out the pastry on a floured surface, and cover the pie in the usual way; make a steam hole. Brush with egg and bake for about 20 minutes until golden, then remove from the oven. Reduce oven to 350°F or Mark 4. Beat the cream with the remaining beaten egg and, using a small funnel, pour into the pie through the steam hole, or carefully lift the edge of the pastry. Shake the pie gently to disperse the mixture. Return to the oven and cook for about a further 15 to 20 minutes to ensure the chicken is cooked through. Serve hot with vegetables or cold with salad. Serves 4 to 6.

Bedruthan Steps, Cornwall

Special Christmas Pudding

Most housewives have their own versions of Christmas pudding, often handed down through the family. This one is full of fruit, contains marmalade and is mixed with stout. The recipe is sufficient to make three 2 lb puddings. Quantities could be halved if required.

½ lb. plain flour   ½ lb. breadcrumbs   1 lb. shredded suet
1 lb. brown sugar   ¾ lb. sultanas   ½ lb. raisins   ¾ lb. currants
1 lb. candied peel   1 teacupful orange marmalade
¼ lb. almonds, blanched and chopped   ¼ lb. glacé cherries
Grated rind of 2 lemons   Juice of 1 lemon
1 teaspoon mixed spice   1 teaspoon salt
6 large eggs   1 glass stout   ½ teaspoon bicarbonate soda

Mix well together all the ingredients, except the stout and bicarbonate of soda and leave covered overnight. Next day, stir again very thoroughly. Butter the pudding basins. Heat the stout and bicarbonate of soda together in a saucepan and add sufficient to the cake mixture while still frothy. The mixture must be stiff and not too moist. Divide the mixture to three-quarters fill the buttered pudding basins and cover with buttered paper and kitchen foil. Put each pudding into a saucepan with sufficient water to come halfway up the basin and boil for 8 hours, topping up the water as necessary. Re-boil for 2 hours on the day the pudding is to be eaten. Serve with plenty of clotted cream.

Bacon and Egg Pie

A shallow pastry-covered tart with sliced sausages in the filling.
A simple and tasty supper dish.

1 lb. shortcrust pastry
2 sausages
3 rashers bacon, de-rinded

2 eggs, beaten
1 tablespoon chopped fresh parsley
Salt and pepper

Set oven to 400°F or Mark 6. Grease an 8-inch sponge tin. Roll out half the pastry on a floured surface and use to line the tin. Cut up the sausages and bacon (either back or streaky) into pieces and arrange over the pastry case. Pour over the beaten eggs. Sprinkle over the chopped parsley and season to taste. Roll out the remaining pastry, cover the pie, seal the edge firmly and make a steam hole. Bake for about 45 minutes until golden brown. Serve cold with a green salad. Serves 3 to 4.

Baked Herrings

Delicately flavoured and inexpensive, herrings make a tasty and nutritious supper dish, excellent eaten hot or cold.

8 herrings	2 or 3 shallots, finely chopped
Salt (preferably sea salt)	4 bay leaves
1 teaspoon ground cloves	Freshly ground black pepper
1 teaspoon allspice	½ pint pale ale

½ pint vinegar

Set oven to 350°F or Mark 4. Clean and fillet the herrings, roll each piece in salt and in the spices and lay in an ovenproof dish. Scatter the finely chopped shallots around the fish and lay the bay leaves on top. Pepper generously. Mix together the ale and vinegar and pour over the fish. Cover with kitchen foil and bake for about 1 hour.

St Mawes, Cornwall

Apple Meringue

This is the Kittow family's favourite pudding.

1 lb. Bramley apples **2 eggs, separated**
Sugar to taste **Zest of 1 orange**
4 oz. caster sugar

Set oven to 300°F or Mark 2. Grease a deep pie dish with butter. Stew the apples with very little water and enough sugar to taste. Separate the egg yolks from the whites. When the apples are cooked, allow to cool before adding the zest from an orange and the egg yolks. Stir well and put into the pie dish. Make the meringue topping by whisking the whites of eggs stiffly, then add half the caster sugar and whisk again until it holds its peaks. Carefully fold in the remainder of the sugar. Spread the meringue over the apple mixture and bake for about 1 hour. Serve cold with Cornish clotted cream, of course! Enough for 4.

Cornish Heavy Cake

Not really a cake but a fruit slice, easily made with rough puff pastry.

1 lb. plain flour
Pinch of salt
3 oz. sultanas
3 oz. currants
2 oz. chopped lemon peel
8 oz. butter
4 oz. lard
Water to mix
Milk for glazing

Set oven to 350°F or Mark 4. Grease and flour a baking sheet. Put the flour, salt, dried fruit and peel into a bowl and add the fats, cut into small pieces. Add enough water to mix to a fairly stiff dough, using a round-bladed knife. Roll out roughly into an oblong on a lightly floured surface and put into the refrigerator to cool for about 10 minutes. Then roll out to about ¾-inch thickness, brush with milk to glaze, put on the baking sheet and bake for about 45 minutes until risen and golden.

METRIC CONVERSIONS

The weights, measures and oven temperatures used in the preceding recipes can be easily converted to their metric equivalents. The conversions listed below are only approximate, having been rounded up or down as may be appropriate.

Weights

Avoirdupois	Metric
1 oz.	just under 30 grams
4 oz. (¼ lb.)	app. 115 grams
8 oz. (½ lb.)	app. 230 grams
1 lb.	454 grams

Liquid Measures

Imperial	Metric
1 tablespoon (liquid only)	20 millilitres
1 fl. oz.	app. 30 millilitres
1 gill (¼ pt.)	app. 145 millilitres
½ pt.	app. 285 millilitres
1 pt.	app. 570 millilitres
1 qt.	app. 1.140 litres

Oven Temperatures

	°Fahrenheit	Gas Mark	°Celsius
Slow	300	2	150
	325	3	170
Moderate	350	4	180
	375	5	190
	400	6	200
Hot	425	7	220
	450	8	230
	475	9	240

Flour as specified in these recipes refers to plain flour unless otherwise described.